Southwest Cookbook

Barbara Karoff

ILLUSTRATED BY
DARLENE CAMPBELL

Chronicle Books

First published in 1993 by
The Appletree Press Ltd
19–21 Alfred Street, Belfast BT2 8DL
Tel. +44 232 243074 Fax +44 232 246756

A Little Southwestern Cookbook

First published in the United States in 1993 by
Chronicle Books, 275 Fifth Street,
San Francisco, California 94103

ISBN 0-8118-0381-3

9 8 7 6 5 4 3 2 1

Introduction

Southwestern fare is strongly rooted in very old Indian, Spanish, and Mexican traditions. Its earthy and robust flavors and unique food combinations are romantic and expressive. Recently, and with good reason, Southwestern foods and cooking traditions have become increasingly popular and well-known beyond their home base.

Tomatoes, garlic, onions, cheese, chilies, tomatillos, beans, avocados, cumin, cilantro, oregano, cinnamon, anise, tortillas, and salsas: these are staples in the Southwestern kitchen. Pinto beans, cumin, and pine nuts are native to the Southwest and corn was cultivated there by the Hopi Indians 2,000 years ago. In New Mexico and Arizona chilies are ubiquitous. Long red chili ropes called ristras adorn adobe walls and hang by doorways. Foods come alive with a variety of flavorful and fiery capsicums. Cilantro compliments and tempers chilies, sweet drinks and desserts balance their spiciness. In any recipe, the number of chilies called for is only a guide. Add or subtract to suit your palate.

Salsas are important and as common on tables as salt and pepper. They may be sharp or sweet, hot or cool, smooth or chunky. Tortillas are almost as important in the southwest as they are in Mexico. Corn tortillas are made with specially prepared cornmeal called masa harina and are usually smaller than the wheat flour variety.

A note on measures

Spoon measures are level. All recipes are for four unless otherwise indicated.

Snacks

Quesadillas

These are filled, rolled and heated tortillas. As is the case with many informal Southwestern dishes, the rules are few and the variations numerous.

Start with flour or corn tortillas. Lay them flat and top each with a generous portion of cooked and seasoned meat or chicken, refried beans, or chilies and cheese. Roll the tortilla around the filling and place it seam side down in a shallow baking dish. Top the tortillas with grated cheese (cheddar, Monterey Jack, munster or a combination) and bake at 375°F for 5 minutes. Serve with salsa and sour cream.

Nachos

A popular snack throughout the Southwest, these are tostadas (crisply fried quarters of corn tortillas) topped with a variety of ingredients which usually include cheese.

Start by frying the tostadas in ¹/₂ inch of hot vegetable oil for 45 to 60 seconds or until they are crisp. Drain them on paper towels, salt them lightly and arrange them on a baking sheet or shallow oven-proof dish. Top with grated cheese (cheddar, Monterey Jack, munster, mozzarella or a combination) and place under the broiler until the cheese is melted. Serve at once or top with any of the following: chili strips, salsa, chopped tomatoes, sliced avocados, chopped green onions, sour cream, guacamole, chili powder, cilantro.

For a more substantial snack, place tostadas on a layer of refried beans before the other ingredients are added.

Salsas

Basic Tomato Sauce or Salsa Cruda

Every cook has his or her own basic tomato sauce. It's used with eggs, vegetables, chilies, chicken, meat, fish, enchiladas, tamales – and other foods as well! The uncooked version is called salsa cruda, or raw sauce. As in any recipe, adjust the heat by the number of chili peppers.

---

2 cloves garlic
1 small onion
2 roasted or canned jalapeño chilis
3 tbsp vegetable oil
2 lbs tomatoes, peeled, chopped
$^1/_2$ tsp oregano
salt to taste
finely chopped cilantro

Mince garlic, onion, and jalapeño chilis. Sauté in oil until soft. Add tomatoes with their juice, oregano and salt. Simmer for 10 to 12 minutes. Cool and stir in cilantro. For Salsa Cruda: Eliminate the oil and sautéeing. Combine all ingredients and let stand for 1 hour at room temperature. Add one or two chopped tomatillos, if desired.

Tomato-Orange Salsa

This simply made salsa is sophisticated and slightly different. It is especially good with black beans, grilled chicken, and sautéed fish.

---
4 green onions, white and green parts, finely minced
2 to 4 jalapeño chilis, seeded, minced
generous pinch of sugar
finely grated peel of one orange
6 tomatoes, peeled, seeded, coarsely chopped
salt to taste

Combine all the ingredients and let stand at room temperature for 2 to 3 hours.

Avocado Salsa Cruda

In the Southwest, salsas are as common on the table as salt and pepper. Every cook has a specialty and not all are hot. Many are chunky and more akin to relishes and most include tomatoes. If fresh tomatoes are not available, use a good quality Italian canned variety.

---
1 avocado, peeled, pitted, diced
1 1/2 cups peeled, seeded, chopped tomatoes
1/2 cup finely diced red onion
1/4 cup seeded, minced jalapeño chili
1/4 cup chopped red bell pepper
1/4 cup minced cilantro or parsley
pinch of sugar
salt to taste

Place diced avocado in a colander and rinse well under cold, running water. Drain. (This prevents avocado from turning dark.) Combine all ingredients and let stand at room temperature for 1 hour.

Jalapeño-Apricot Jelly

The dried fruit in this sparkling sweet-hot jelly adds an intriguing dimension to what has become a Southwestern classic.   Dried peaches or nectarines can be substituted for apricots.   Serve the jelly with grilled red meats or chicken.

---

1 cup red or green bell pepper chunks
2 cups cider vinegar
$^1/_3$ cup fresh jalapeño chilis, stems and seeds removed
1 $^1/_4$ cups dried apricots, finely slivered
6 cups sugar
3 oz liquid pectin
5 drops red or green food coloring

Purée the peppers, vinegar, and jalapeño chilis in a blender or food processor.   Do not liquefy completely.   Combine the apricots, sugar, and ground peppers in a pan and boil 5 minutes. Remove from the heat and skim off foam.   Cool 2 minutes. Add pectin and red or green food coloring (depending on color of bell pepper used.) Pour into hot sterilized jars and seal.

Southwest Chili Soufflé Pie

This quickly prepared and attractive breakfast dish is also satisfying for lunch, supper, or as a snack. Red bell pepper strips can be added to or substituted for the jalapeño chilis.

---

2 cups grated cheddar cheese
6 large eggs, beaten until frothy
2 to 4 fresh jalapeño chilis

Lightly oil a 9-inch pie plate. Cover the bottom with grated cheese. Remove stems and seeds from the jalapeño chilis and cut into thin strips. Arrange strips decoratively on top of the cheese. Pour beaten eggs over. Bake at 275°F for 45 minutes. Serve warm.

Huevos Rancheros

Served with a steaming cup of cinnamon-laced Mexican chocolate, ranch eggs are a breakfast treat. With an icy cold beer, they are good anytime. Originally, the eggs were poached in the salsa — still a flavorful method. Refried beans and spicy sausage are traditional accompaniments.

---

4 corn tortillas	2 cups Basic Tomato Sauce,
1 tbsp vegetable oil	warmed (see p. 7)
1 tbsp butter, melted	1 cup grated Monterey Jack
4 large eggs, poached,	or cheddar cheese
fried or scrambled	1 avocado, peeled, pitted,
	sliced

Heat tortillas in oil and butter and drain on paper towels. Place each tortilla on a warmed plate and top with an egg. Spoon salsa over and top with cheese and avocado.

Refried Beans

Refried beans are almost as popular in the Southwest as they are in Mexico. They accompany Huevos Rancheros (see p. 12), fill tacos and burritos, and go well with grilled meats. In fact, they turn up everywhere on a menu. Garnish them, if you like, with sliced avocado, grated cheese, or salsa. Pinto beans are the most popular, but white pea beans and black beans are excellent, too.

---

2 $\frac{1}{2}$ tbsp vegetable oil or bacon drippings
2 cups cooked beans with some liquid

Heat the oil in a heavy skillet. Add the beans and mash them with a potato masher. Heat and stir until the beans are heated and slightly dried.

Cheese Soup

In Spanish this soup is called Sopa de Queso. It's a perfect beginning to any informal meal.

1 onion, chopped	³/₄ cup chopped green chilies
2 cloves garlic, minced	2 cups cream-style corn
1 red bell pepper, seeded, chopped	2 new potatoes, cooked, diced
1 tbsp vegetable oil	1 cup grated Monterey Jack cheese
7 cups chicken stock	

Sauté onion, garlic, and bell pepper in oil until soft. Heat stock and add sautéed vegetables, green chilies, corn and potatoes. Simmer 5 minutes. Stir in the cheese and serve at once.

Cream of Green Chili Soup

This traditional Southwestern soup calls for mild Anaheim chilies and so is not as hot as the numbers might indicate. Add a jalapeño chili or two if more heat is desired.

6 cups chicken stock
3 onions
4 cloves garlic
10 to 15 Anaheim chilies, seeded
1 tbsp ground cumin
3 cups half-and-half, approximately
cilantro

In batches, purée onions, garlic, and chilies with stock in a blender or food processor. Pour purée into a pan, add cumin and heat just to a boil. Simmer 5 minutes. Let cool. Stir in half-and-half to pouring consistency and correct seasoning. Serve hot or cold garnished with cilantro.

Corn Soup

This soup, with its south-of-the-border flavors, is popular throughout the Southwest. Served with tostadas and a green salad, it makes a complete meal.

---

3 $1/2$ cups corn kernels, preferably fresh
I cup chicken stock
2 tbsp butter
2 cups milk
I clove garlic, minced
I tsp oregano
salt and pepper
2 tbsp canned green chilies, diced, drained
I cup peeled, seeded, chopped tomato
I cup cubed Monterey Jack cheese

Purée corn and stock in a blender or food processor. Place purée in a saucepan with butter. Stir and simmer 5 minutes. Add milk, garlic, oregano, salt and pepper and bring to a boil. Reduce heat, add chilies, simmer 5 minutes. Divide tomatoes among 4 soup bowls. Remove soup from heat and add cheese. Stir until just melted. Ladle over tomatoes in bowls.

Avocado Soup

In this refreshing cold soup, grapefruit juice is an excellent contrast to the rich avocados. For best results, use freshly squeezed juice and black-skinned Haas avocados.

3 ripe avocados	salt and pepper
2 cups chicken stock	chopped cilantro
1 cup grapefruit juice	

Peel and seed avocados. Purée them in a blender or food processor with the stock and juice. Add salt and pepper and more stock or juice to taste. Serve chilled, garnished with cilantro.

Tamale Pie

Tamale Pie is another dish of which the variations are legion. Some use leftover meat, some call for chicken and others for red meat or sausage. All are delicious. Whatever filling you choose, serve the finished pie with a salsa.

2 tbsp finely chopped onion	salt and pepper
2 tbsp finely chopped bell pepper	1 cup cream style corn
2 tbsp vegetable oil	1/2 cup black olives, cut in half
1/2 cup chopped green chilies	1 cup yellow cornmeal
2 cups cooked chicken, cut up	1/2 tsp chili powder
3 tomatoes, peeled, seeded, chopped	3/4 cup grated Monterey Jack cheese

Sauté onion and bell pepper in oil until soft. Add green chilies, chicken, tomatoes, salt, pepper, corn and olives.

Stir well and set aside. Mix cornmeal with 1 cup water. Bring 3 cups water to a boil. Add chili powder and cornmeal-water mixture and cook and stir for 5 minutes. Line a buttered baking dish with half the cornmeal. Fill with chicken mixture and spread remaining cornmeal over the top. Sprinkle with cheese. Bake at 350°F for 20 minutes.

Chilies Rellenos

Traditionally, Chilies Rellenos are deep fried. In this lighter version the flavor remains, and the messy frying is eliminated. Canned chilies can be substituted if fresh are not available. This dish is especially attractive made in individual gratin dishes allowing 2 chilies per person.

---

1 ½ cups half-and-half
3 large eggs
½ cup flour
8 whole roasted Anaheim chilies
¾ lb Monterey Jack or cheddar cheese, grated
1 ½ cups salsa or tomato sauce (see p. 7)
cilantro

Beat half-and-half with eggs and flour until smooth. Split chilies, rinse away seeds and drain on paper towels. Set aside ⅔ cup cheese. In a buttered casserole dish make alternate layers of cheese, chilies and egg mixture. Top with salsa or tomato sauce and sprinkle with reserved cheese. Bake at 350°F for 45 minutes. Serve hot garnished with cilantro.

Chili with Avocados

There are probably as many chili recipes as there are chili cooks. This version, without beans and served in avocado halves, is an informally elegant and festive main dish. Serve it with Old Southwestern Spoon Bread (see p. 51).

---

3 onions, coarsely chopped
4 cloves garlic, chopped
3 tbsp vegetable oil
2 lbs beef round, cut in small cubes
I lb lean pork, cut in small cubes
$1/3$ cup chili powder
I tbsp flour
I large can Italian tomatoes, cut up, with juice
3 bay leaves
salt
I tbsp oregano
2 tsp ground cumin
I tbsp brown sugar
I tbsp red wine vinegar
I cup pimento-stuffed green olives, drained
3 avocados, peeled, halved

In a medium saucepan sauté onion and garlic in oil until soft. Remove and set aside. Brown meat over high heat in same pan. Stir in onions, garlic, chili powder, flour, tomatoes, bay leaves, oregano, cumin, sugar, salt, and vinegar. Bring to a boil, lower heat and simmer covered for 2 hours, stirring occasionally. Discard bay leaves. Stir in olives, correct seasoning, and serve over avocado halves.

Posole

More subtle than Chili, and equally addictive, the dish called Posole is a pork and/or chicken and hominy stew and is truly representative of the Southwest where it is often served on Christmas Eve. To make red (and hot) Posole, add dried red chili pods to the pots when cooking the meats. The many festive garnishes are traditional.

I lb boneless pork, fat trimmed, cut in cubes
6 chicken thighs, skin removed
I onion, chopped
2 cloves garlic
I tbsp salt
12 whole peppercorns
3 cups hominy, fresh, frozen or canned
4 red chili pods (optional)

Simmer pork in water to cover with half the onion, garlic, salt, and peppercorns. Simmer chicken in water to cover with remaining onion, garlic, salt, and peppercorns. Skim, if necessary and simmer until each is tender. Place meats in a large pot, removing chicken from bones. Add hominy. Strain both broths and add. Simmer 30 minutes. Serve in large bowls and pass garnishes: salsa, minced onion, sliced radishes, shredded iceberg lettuce, dry oregano, lime wedges, sliced avocados.

Basic Black Beans

Black beans have an intense, rich flavor all their own and are especially delicious when combined with ham or sausage. Serve this dish as an entrée along with a lettuce and grapefruit salad and a light dessert or, omit the ham hocks, and serve the beans as a side dish.

---

2 cups black beans, washed and picked over
2 meaty ham hocks
2 tbsp vegetable oil
2 onions, diced
4 cloves garlic, minced
2 to 4 jalapeño chilis, seeded, minced
1 cup chopped cilantro

Bring beans and ham hocks to a boil in water to cover. Simmer until beans are tender but not mushy — about 1 hour. Sauté onions, garlic and jalapeño chilis in oil until very soft. Drain beans. Remove meat from ham hocks and add meat to beans along with sautéed vegetables. Salt to taste. Top with chopped cilantro.

Chili-Corn Soufflé

This light entrée is a sophisticated blend of Southwestern flavors. If fresh corn is not available, frozen is the next best.

---

3 tbsp butter
3 green onions, white and green, minced
3 tbsp flour
I cup milk
4 large egg yolks
salt and pepper
4 jalapeño chilis, seeded, minced
I 1/2 cups corn kernels, preferably fresh
I 1/2 tsp chopped fresh basil
I cup grated cheddar cheese
6 large egg whites

Melt butter in a large saucepan and sauté onions until soft. Stir in flour and cook 2 minutes. Stir in milk and whisk until smooth and thickened — 6 to 7 minutes. Cool slightly. Add egg yolks, whisk to blend. Stir in salt, pepper, jalapeño chilis, corn, basil, and cheddar. Beat egg whites until stiff but not dry and fold into chili-corn mixture in three parts. Pour into deep, buttered gratin or quiche dish and bake at 450°F for about 20 minutes. Serve immediately.

Carne Asada

Carne Asada means grilled or barbecued meat and the key to successful barbecuing is a hot fire and direct heat. In the Southwestern tradition, serve the meat with salsa, tortillas, beans (freshly cooked or refried), guacamole, and rice. If a barbecue is not available, pan fry the meat quickly over high heat.

2 lbs skirt steak, well trimmed	2 tbsp vegetable oil
juice of 6 limes	2 cloves garlic, minced

Cut the meat into 4-inch lengths and marinate the strips in lime juice, oil, and garlic for 20 minutes. Grill over hot coals or pan fry in a small amount of additional oil if necessary. Either cooking method should take less than 1 minute.

Tortilla Casserole

The flavors of the Southwest come alive in this hearty casserole. Other beans besides black beans may be used.

10 corn tortillas, torn into pieces	1/2 tsp oregano
	salt and pepper
2 cloves garlic, minced	2 cups canned Italian tomatoes, cut up, with juice
1 large onion, diced	
1 red bell pepper, seeded, diced	1 cup sour cream
2 jalapeño chilis, seeded, minced	1 cup cooked black beans
	1 cup grated Monterey Jack
1 lb lean, ground pork	or cheddar cheese

Sauté garlic, onion, bell pepper, jalapeño chilis, and pork until vegetables are soft and meat is no longer pink. Add salt, pepper, and oregano and set aside. Combine tomatoes and sour cream and set aside. Lightly oil a 2 qt. casserole dish.

Cover bottom of dish with $1/3$ of tortillas. Cover with $1/2$ the meat mixture. Add another $1/3$ tortillas. Add all the tomato mixture and top with remaining meat. Top with all the beans. Finish with remaining tortillas and finally the cheese. Bake at 350°F for 25 minutes or until heated through.

Burritos

Southwestern meals and entertaining are often informal and Burritos are a casual do-it-yourself meal that is easily prepared and delicious to eat anytime.

I cup finely chopped onions
2 tbsp vegetable oil
4 cups refried beans (see p. 15)
8 warm flour tortillas
1 $1/2$ cups grated Monterey Jack or cheddar cheese

Sauté onion in oil a large skillet until soft. Add the beans, mix well and heat through. Place a large spoonful of beans on each tortilla. Top with cheese. Add one or all of the following: salsa, guacamole or sliced avocados, chopped tomato, cooked chopped chicken or meat, sour cream. Fold the bottom of the tortilla over the filling, fold in sides and top. Serve at once with additional salsa.

Southwestern Enchiladas

Enchiladas are corn tortillas, either yellow or blue, plus fillings, plus garnishes. They are good anytime and are especially handy when a quick meal is in order.

Allow about 3 tortillas per serving and have fillings and garnishes ready. Dip tortillas in hot oil to soften and then press between paper towels or steam them in a colander over simmering water. Spoon filling onto each tortilla, roll it and place seam side down on a baking sheet or stack 3 tortillas for each person with filling between each layer. Place stack on baking sheet. Bake at 350°F for 10 to 15 minutes. Use fillings and garnishes as desired.

Fillings
Grated cheese, chopped onion, bell peppers, chilies, tomatoes, cooked meat or chicken, refried beans. Garnishes: salsa, avocado, sour cream, olives.

Green Chili Stew

Green Chili Stew is an old New Mexican staple which can be prepared with lamb, beef, or pork. The Navajo Indians use lamb, but a combination of beef and pork is good, too. It's a fine dish to prepare a day in advance because it tastes even better the second day.

1 1/2 lbs lean meat, cut in cubes	1/2 cup water
2 tbsp vegetable oil	4 zucchini, cut in chunks
1 large red onion, chopped	1 tsp oregano
4 cups water	2 cloves garlic, minced
4 potatoes, quartered	1 small potato, grated
1/2 to 1 cup green chilies, seeded, cut up	salt and pepper
1 cup cilantro	sour cream (optional)

In a large saucepan brown the meat in oil. Add onion and continue cooking until onion is soft. Deglaze pan with 2 cups water. Add remaining water and simmer covered for 30 minutes. Add the quartered potatoes and continue cooking until the meat and potatoes are tender. In a blender or food processor purée the chilies, cilantro and 1/2 cup water. Add to the meat along with zucchini, oregano, garlic, grated potato, salt and pepper. Cook 15 minutes. Serve in large bowls. If desired, top with sour cream.

Chili con Queso

This fondue-like dish is fun for a few friends to sit around the table and eat together. A mixed green salad and a plate of crudités are perfect accompaniments.

---

2 tbsp vegetable oil
I cup chopped onions
I clove garlic, pressed
2 large tomatoes, peeled, seeded, coarsely chopped
$^3/_4$ cup canned green chilies, chopped
2 cups grated Monterey Jack cheese
$^1/_2$ cup sour cream or heavy cream
tostadas

In a large skillet, sauté onion and garlic in oil until the onion is soft. Add tomatoes, chilies, and cheese and stir over low heat until cheese is melted. Transfer the mixture to a chafing dish over hot water or to a fondue pot over a warmer. Stir in sour or heavy cream and serve at once with tostadas for dipping.

Red and Green Chili Slaw

This attractive slaw is especially good with bean dishes. Regulate the heat by the choice of and number of chilies.

---

3 green chilies, seeded, minced
1/4 head green cabbage, shredded
1/4 head red cabbage, shredded
4 green onions, white and green, minced
1/2 cup mayonnaise
1 tbsp sugar
1 tbsp white wine vinegar
salt and pepper
pinch of chili powder

Combine first 4 ingredients and set aside. Combine remaining ingredients and set aside. Combine two mixtures just before serving and garnish with cilantro, if desired.

Pico de Gallo

The name of this refreshing salad means "beak of the rooster". Traditionally, it is prepared with jicama, a brown-skinned root vegetable similar in appearance to a potato but similar in texture to a cucumber which can be substituted. Black olives and slices of apple or pineapple are sometimes added.

---

4 eating oranges
2 red bell peppers
1 small jicama

Over a bowl, peel oranges, remove membrane and seeds, and cut sections into thirds. Save the juice in the bowl. In another bowl, combine the orange sections with the bell peppers, seeded and diced finely, and the peeled jicama cut in short julienne. To the orange juice, add:

$1/3$ cup olive oil
$1/4$ cup white wine vinegar
$1/4$ tsp chili powder
1 clove garlic, pressed
dash of sugar
salt and pepper

Whisk the dressing ingredients together and combine with the chopped ingredients just before serving. Serve on lettuce leaves.

Blue Corn Bread

Blue cornmeal, a long time favorite in the Southwest, is more flavorful than the yellow or white varieties. Because this bread dries out quickly, it is best eaten the day it is baked.

---

1 1/2 cups blue cornmeal
3 tbsp sugar
2 tsp baking powder
3/4 cup milk
1 large egg, beaten
3 tbsp bacon drippings, melted
3 tbsp minced green chilies (optional)

In a large bowl, combine the dry ingredients. In another bowl combine the milk, egg, drippings, and chilies and add them to the dry ingredients. Mix just enough to combine. Pour into greased 8 inch square or round pan and bake at 350°F for about 20 minutes. Take care not to over bake.

Blue Corn Muffins

These excellent muffins are light and moist and actually more gray in color than true blue. The blue corn, from which the meal is ground, has religious significance for the Southwestern Indians who have grown it for centuries.

---

1 1/2 cups white flour
1 cup blue cornmeal
3 tsp baking powder
1 tsp baking soda
1 tsp sugar
1 1/2 cups milk
2 large eggs, well beaten
1/3 cup vegetable oil

In a large bowl, combine the dry ingredients. In another bowl, combine the milk, eggs, and oil and add them to the dry ingredients. Mix just enough to combine. Fill well-greased muffin pans two thirds full and bake at 400°F for about 20 minutes. Makes 12 regular size muffins.

Old Southwest Spoon Bread

This "corn bread in a casserole" is lighter and more soufflé-like than regular corn bread and is just the right texture to be eaten with a spoon. It goes well with black beans, meats, and chili and is also good for breakfast.

---

1 cup milk
1/2 cup yellow cornmeal
1/2 tsp salt
2 tbsp butter or bacon drippings
2 large eggs, separated
1/4 cup minced onion
1 jalapeño chili, seeded, minced
1/2 cup grated cheddar cheese (optional)

Heat milk in top of a double boiler until almost boiling. Add cornmeal slowly, stirring constantly. Cook about 1 minute – until thick and smooth. Don't allow it to become too thick. Add salt and butter. Cool. Beat egg yolks and add along with onion, jalapeño chili, and cheese. Beat whites until stiff but not dry and fold in. Pour into well-buttered 1 qt. casserole dish and bake at 375°F for 35 to 40 minutes or until puffed and brown. Serve hot with butter.

Avocado Ice Cream

This delicate pale green dessert pleasantly surprises people when they taste it for the first time and almost always brings them back for more.

---

1 1/2 cups milk
1/4 cup sugar
1/4 tbsp cornstarch
1/2 tbsp water
1 large egg
1/4 cup heavy cream
1 large ripe avocado, peeled, pitted
2 tsp orange juice
1/2 tsp grated orange peel, orange part only
1 tbsp powdered sugar

Bring milk and sugar to a boil. Combine the cornstarch and water and add to the milk. Continue to boil gently for 3 minutes. Remove from heat and cool to warm. Beat the egg and pour the milk over it, combining well. Strain and add the cream. Mash the avocado with the orange juice, peel, and powdered sugar. Press through a sieve and add to the custard. Freeze in freezer compartment or in an ice cream freezer.

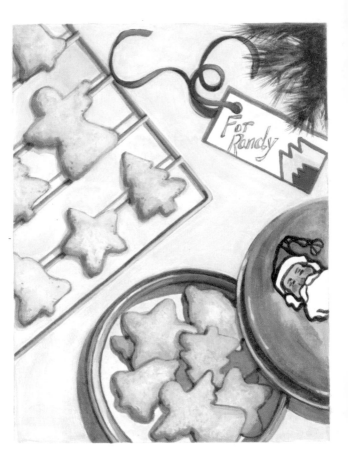

Biscochitos

Biscochitos are traditional New Mexican Christmas cookies with a delightful elusive flavor and many variations. The chilled dough can also be rolled to a thickness of $1/4$ inch and cut into shapes with cookie cutters.

---

1 cup pine nuts
1 cup soft butter
$3/4$ cup sugar
2 large egg yolks
2 tsp anise seeds, slightly crushed
2 $1/4$ cups flour
$1/8$ tsp baking powder
$1/4$ tsp salt
(makes 50)

Toast pine nuts in a 375°F oven for 4 to 5 minutes. Watch carefully and do not allow to become too brown. In a medium-size bowl cream butter and sugar together until light. Add the egg yolks, and anise seeds and mix well. In another bowl, combine the flour, baking powder, and salt and add to the creamed mixture. Blend well and stir in pine nuts. Form dough into three 2 inch diameter logs. Wrap in plastic wrap and chill 1 hour or more. Cut logs into $1/4$-inch slices and bake on ungreased sheet at 350°F for about 8 minutes until just lightly browned. Remove to racks immediately.

Buttermilk Pie

This quite sweet pie is especially good topped with fresh fruit. Sliced peaches or nectarines or any fresh berries are a good choice.

1 unbaked 8-inch pie shell	2 eggs
2 tbsp butter	$1/2$ tsp vanilla extract
$2/3$ cup sugar	$1/4$ tsp lemon extract
2 tbsp flour	$1/2$ cup buttermilk

In a medium-size bowl cream butter and sugar together until light. Add the flour and combine thoroughly. Add the eggs, one at a time, beating well after each addition. Add the extracts and the buttermilk and pour into pie shell. Bake at 425°F for 10 minutes. Reduce heat to 350°F and continue to bake for 30 minutes or until the custard is set. Serve warm with fruit.

Spiced Coffee

This unusual after dinner drink will take the chill off any evening. Biscochitos are the perfect companion.

---

²/₃ cup brown sugar, firmly packed
3 cinnamon sticks
6 whole cloves
2 allspice berries
6 tbsp regular grind coffee (not instant)
6 strips orange zest or lightly whipped cream

Heat 6 cups of water with the brown sugar, cinnamon, cloves and allspice. When it is just at a boil, add the coffee and boil gently, stirring occasionally, for 4 minutes. Strain into warmed cups and garnish with orange zest or whipped cream.

Sangria

Sangria is of Spanish origin and very popular in the Southwest. It's refreshing any place and time when the weather is hot. The better the wine, the better the drink.

---

2 cups fresh squeezed orange juice	3 cups red wine
	¹/₃ cup sugar, or to taste
¹/₄ cup fresh squeezed lemon juice	mint sprigs

Combine juices, wine, and sugar. Chill well and pour into tall ice-filled glasses to serve. Garnish with mint.

Index